MR. BEAN'S HOLIDAY

Based on the original character created by Rowan Atkinson & Richard Curtis

Based on the motion picture screenplay by Hamish McColl and Robin Driscoll

CB003189

LEVEL 1

SCHOLASTIC

Adapted by: Paul Shipton
Publisher: Jacquie Bloese
Editor: Matthew Hancock
Cover design: Dawn Wilson
Designer: Dawn Wilson
Picture research: Emma Bree
Photo credits:
Cover and interior photos courtesy of
Copyright © Universal Studios, 2007
Page 5: PHB/isifa Image Service s.r.o./Alamy.
Page 8: R. Cooke/Alamy.
Page 33: Tiger Aspect.
Pages 34 & 35: A. C. Poujoulat/AFP, M. J. Kim/Getty Images;
Allstar.
Pages 36 & 37: Photodisc; D. Hallinan, H. Kurihara/Alamy;
A. Julien/AFP/Getty Images; R. Young/Rex.
Character © Tiger Aspect Productions Limited, 2007

Published by Scholastic Ltd 2007

No part of this publication may be reproduced in whole or
in part, or stored in a retrieval system, or transmitted in any
form or by any means, electronic, mechanical, photocopying,
recording or otherwise, without the written permission of
the publisher. For information regarding permission write to:

Mary Glasgow Magazines (Scholastic Ltd.)
Euston House
24 Eversholt Street
London NW1 IDB

Printed in Malaysia.

Reprinted in 2008, 2009, 2010, 2011, 2012, 2014, 2016, 2017 and 2018

Contents

MR BEAN

Mr Bean lives alone in London. He is very happy because he is going to have a beach holiday in France. But nothing is easy for Mr Bean. There are going to be problems on the way!

SABINE

Sabine is a pretty French actress. She wants to be a famous film star. Her first part is in Carson Clay's new film.

STEPAN

Stepan is a boy from Russia. His father is a famous film-maker. They are going from Paris to the film festival in Cannes, but then they meet Mr Bean …

CARSON CLAY

Carson Clay is a famous American actor and film-maker. He is going to show his new film at the Cannes Film Festival. He loves the films … of Carson Clay!

PLACES

London
The biggest city in Britain is Mr Bean's home. He loves the city, but he doesn't like all the rain there!

Paris
Mr Bean goes to Paris by train from London. Mr Bean does not find it easy to go through this big city. And he does not understand the French, or their food.

Cannes
Cannes is a beautiful French town with a lot of beaches. Every May, there is a famous film festival.

CHAPTER 1
First prize

The London weather was terrible – dark skies and rain. A LOT of rain.

Mr Bean ran from his little car into the church. There were a lot of people there because the church needed money. Some people bought cakes or books; some played games. Mr Bean was there for the competition. The first prize was a holiday in France *and* a fantastic video camera!

'And the prize goes to the person with this number …' said the man at the front. Mr Bean looked at his ticket. He wanted that prize!

'… 919!'

Mr Bean looked at his ticket again. He had number 616. He was not happy – no fun in the sun for Mr Bean!

He didn't need this stupid ticket now. There was a boy in front of him with a little train. Mr Bean put the ticket on top of the train.

'Does anyone have ticket number 919?' asked the man at the front.

No one answered. Mr Bean watched as the boy's train went around and around with his ticket. And then he saw it – his ticket wasn't number 616! It was number 919!

'Anyone?' asked the man for the last time.

Mr Bean was fast. He had the ticket back in his hand.

'I'm going to go to France!' he thought. 'I'm going to go to the beach in Cannes!'

* * *

Mr Bean was on the train to Paris. This was exciting! It was his first time in France. He went to the bar.

'Do you want a coffee?' the woman asked in French.

Mr Bean was ready. He knew the French word for 'yes'.

'*Oui*!' he said.

'Sugar?' asked the woman.

Mr Bean smiled. He knew the French for 'no', too.

'*Non*.'

'You speak good French,' said the woman in French.

Mr Bean was happy. 'I am going to have a fantastic holiday,' he thought.

'*Gracias*,' he said to the woman and walked away. The woman looked at him. 'Why is he speaking in Spanish?' she thought.

CHAPTER 2
Where's the station?

At the train station in Paris, Mr Bean filmed everything with his new video camera. But the train to Cannes left from a different station.

'I can take a taxi!' thought Mr Bean.

The taxis were in front of the station. Mr Bean told the driver the name of his station and then he turned for his bags. But he was too slow. A man got into the taxi and it drove away. Mr Bean didn't see this. He didn't see the second taxi as it moved up.

A different man said something to the second taxi driver and then turned to his wife. Mr Bean didn't see *this* and got into the back of the second taxi. And so it took Mr Bean … to the wrong place.

Mr Bean looked around. He didn't understand. Where was the station? Where were the trains? Suddenly he knew – he was in the wrong place!

Mr Bean tried to ask someone for help. He walked up to a man and tried to make the sound of a train. 'Choo, choo!' he said. The man walked away quickly.

Then Mr Bean saw a map of Paris. The right station wasn't *very* far.

'I'm going to walk there!' thought Mr Bean.

Mr Bean started to walk. He didn't want to go the wrong way and so he used a compass. He didn't turn and he didn't stop. He didn't even look up from the compass. He came to a road but he didn't stop. A car almost hit him, then a second car. Drivers shouted angrily, but Mr Bean didn't hear them. There was just one thought in his head: 'I am going to reach that station!'

* * *

Carson Clay was an American actor and film-maker. There were a lot of people around him. They all wanted photos and stories about him for their newspapers.

'How long are you going to be in France?' one man asked him.

'I'm going to be in Cannes on Sunday with my new film,' said Carson. 'Before that, I'm going to work with this great actress, Sylvie.'

'My name is Sabine,' said a young woman with him.

Everyone tried to take photos of Clay, but there was a problem. Someone was in front of him – an English man with a compass and his head down …

Mr Bean walked and walked. Then at last he looked up and smiled. He was at the station!

CHAPTER 3
Train problems

Mr Bean was hungry after his walk. There was a little time before his train left. He put some money into a vending machine. The machine took his money … and the end of his tie, too. It started to pull the tie up. Now Mr Bean's face was against the front of the machine.

He heard something. 'My train is leaving!' he thought. He pulled and pulled. The machine was strong, but Mr Bean pulled his tie out. He ran … but he was too late. He watched as the train to Cannes left the station.

***

Mr Bean was ready for the next train.

This was exciting! He asked a man to film him as he got on the train. The man put down the drinks in his hand and took the video camera.

Mr Bean smiled for the camera and walked slowly to the train. The man tried to film this but something was in the way.

'Again!' said Mr Bean. He walked to the door again, but this time he walked into the man's drinks.

'Again!'

Mr Bean smiled for the camera. Yes, everything was OK! He took the camera back and got on the train.

The man turned and picked up his drinks. But suddenly the train doors closed.

'Open the door!' he shouted to Mr Bean.

But it was not possible to open the door now. The train started to move.

The man ran next to the train and shouted, 'Stop!'

Mr Bean filmed him with his video camera.

A boy on the train started to shout to the man. He was frightened. The man was his father and he wasn't on the train!

'Get off at the next station,' the man shouted to the boy in Russian.

Mr Bean sat opposite the Russian boy and smiled.

The boy, Stepan, gave him a long, cold look. He was alone in France because of this stupid man.

Mr Bean moved his ears up and down.

Stepan just looked.

Mr Bean started to make funny faces.

The boy hit him.

***

At the next station, Mr Bean woke up and looked out of the window. The boy was off the train now. He sat alone and waited for his father.

But then a big man with a drink in one hand started to talk to the boy. Mr Bean didn't like the look of this. He ran off the train and gave the man a long look.

The man walked slowly away and Mr Bean got back onto the train. He looked at the boy and started to say goodbye. Then he saw something in the boy's hand – his video camera!

Mr Bean ran off the train for his camera, but then – oh no! – the train started to leave. He turned, but it was too late. The door did not open.

Mr Bean watched as the train left the station … with all of his bags on it!

CHAPTER 4
More train problems

Mr Bean was not happy. Now he had his video camera but no bags.

He and Stepan waited. Suddenly they heard something – the next train! Was Stepan's father on it?

He was, but there was a problem.

'The train isn't stopping!' shouted Stepan in Russian.

Suddenly he saw his father at a window in the train. He had a bit of paper with the word CANNES and a telephone number on it. He wanted his son to call him on his mobile phone in Cannes. But it wasn't possible for Stepan to write the number!

Mr Bean had an idea. He pulled out his camera and ran. As he ran, he filmed Stepan's father on the train.

Mr Bean and Stepan watched the film on the video camera's little screen. They saw Stepan's father with the telephone number. But there was a problem.

'We can't read the last two numbers,' said Stepan in Russian. 'His hand is over them!'

Mr Bean started to write all the possible numbers: 0608080700, 0608080701, 0608080702 … There were a lot.

Stepan started to call the numbers. But it was not easy; he didn't speak French.

The first telephone number was wrong. The second number was wrong, too. And the next …

Suddenly, Stepan and Mr Bean looked around. A train was at the station – a train to Cannes. They ran to the open doors.

They sat down and the train went. Mr Bean looked out of the window and saw his wallet. It was still on top of the telephone at the station! Now he had no money … and no train ticket.

'Tickets, please,' said a ticket inspector.

Oh no! Mr Bean told Stepan to go under his chair. He ran to a different part of the train. He went into a little bathroom and closed the door. Then he looked around … A man was already in there!

'Sorry!' Mr Bean opened the door quickly. The ticket inspector was there with an angry look on her face.

At the next station, she pulled Mr Bean and Stepan off the train. Now they had no bags, no tickets and no money.

'How do we go to Cannes now?' thought Mr Bean.

CHAPTER 5
Music and money

Mr Bean and Stepan went into the town. The streets and shops were busy with a lot of people.

Mr Bean heard music. Some musicians were in the street. Mr Bean watched as people gave them money. This gave Mr Bean an idea.

He was next to a little CD shop. When Shaggy's* *Mr Bombastic* started, Mr Bean started to dance. A lot of people looked at him, but no one gave any money.

Then some different music started. It was a beautiful, sad song and Mr Bean started to move his mouth to the words. With some black clothes on his head, he acted the story of the music. More and more people started to watch him act.

Now Mr Bean had Stepan in his arms. Mr Bean was the mother and Stepan was her son. The "mother" sat and cried over her "son's" dead body. The music ended and everything was quiet. And then all the people started to shout for Mr Bean. They loved him! They started to give him money.

* Shaggy is a Jamaican reggae singer.

* * *

Now Mr Bean and Stepan had bags and bags of food. And they had two bus tickets for Cannes.

'I'm going to see my father soon!' thought Stepan.

'I'm going to see the beach!' thought Mr Bean.

The Russian boy got on the bus. Mr Bean was behind him with the ticket in his mouth.

'Cannes?' asked the bus driver.

'*Oui*,' answered Mr Bean.

The ticket! It was on the floor of the bus now. Mr Bean put down his bags of food and tried to get it, but there was a strong wind that day. Now the ticket was on the road! Mr Bean followed it.

Stepan watched from the bus as Mr Bean ran faster and faster after the ticket. Suddenly the wind stopped. The ticket was next to some chickens. Then one of the chickens walked over it. Now the bus ticket was on the chicken's left foot!

Mr Bean tried to take it, but that chicken was fast. Where was it? Mr Bean looked here, he looked there. No chicken. And then he saw a man put it with a lot of other chickens. Then the man started to drive away.

But that chicken still had Mr Bean's bus ticket!

There was a bicycle next to a café. Mr Bean took it. He started to ride after the man and his chickens.

'I must have that ticket!' thought Mr Bean.

CHAPTER 6
On the road

Mr Bean was in the country now, but he did not stop. He wanted that ticket!

A car came and Mr Bean had one hand on it. The car pulled him fast down the road. The car turned and now Mr Bean was by a big country house. He heard the sound of chickens. Yes! The chickens – and the ticket – were here.

He ran to an old building and opened the door. There were chickens everywhere. But where was the chicken with the ticket?

'I'm never going to find it!' thought Mr Bean.

Sadly he walked back to the bicycle. But there was a problem. The bicycle was flat in the road. It wasn't possible to ride it now. What happened?

Mr Bean took the video camera from the front of the bicycle and looked at the little screen. He watched as a big tank drove down the road and then on top of the bicycle. A tank!

So Mr Bean had no bus ticket, no money and no bicycle.

What now? There was only one answer. He waited next to the long, empty road.

'A car is going to come soon,' he thought.

After a few minutes, he saw something far away. It wasn't a car. It was a little moped!

Mr Bean waited.

And waited.

And waited. He looked at his watch. This moped was very slow. The man on it was big. After a few more minutes, he arrived at Mr Bean and stopped the moped. Mr Bean sat on the back and the moped started again.

But two men were too much for the little moped. The big man stopped. He started to look at the moped.

But Mr Bean did not want to wait any more. Quickly he took the moped and started to ride away!

Mr Bean didn't remember one thing. This little moped was very slow. Someone was now behind him. It was the big French man – the owner of the moped. He walked faster than the moped! The angry man took his moped back.

Now Mr Bean was alone again. There were no cars … nothing.

It was a long way to Cannes, but Mr Bean started to walk. At the end of the day, he was very tired. He remembered nothing after that.

CHAPTER 7
Bean the soldier

Mr Bean woke up. Slowly he remembered his long walk yesterday. Now it was the next morning.

He looked around. He was in a beautiful little French town with a nice little café. A young woman had some drinks in her hand. A few older people sat at tables. Some children played and laughed. Everything looked beautiful.

But suddenly there was a different sound. A big tank drove into the town! BOOM! There was a big explosion. Then some German soldiers followed the tank and ran into the town.

Mr Bean watched with big eyes. 'What is happening?'

He saw the young woman at the café again.

'I must help her!' he thought. He ran to the woman and pulled her away from the soldiers.

'Stop!' someone shouted. All the soldiers stopped. 'Who is that man? Where did he come from?'

It was Carson Clay, the American film-maker. This was one of his films!

He looked at Mr Bean. 'He's in the wrong clothes,' said Clay. 'Give him some soldiers' clothes. Then we can film again!'

Mr Bean wasn't one of the actors, but the film-maker didn't know this. Someone pulled his arm and Mr Bean followed.

* * *

Carson Clay was behind the camera and ready to film again. The German soldiers ran into the little town, but now Mr Bean was one of them!

'Stop!' shouted Carson Clay angrily. 'That soldier has got a video camera with him!'

All the soldiers stopped again.

'You're off this film!' Clay shouted at Mr Bean. 'Go!'

Mr Bean started to leave, but first he needed to do something.

'My video camera is not working,' he thought. 'I need to plug it in.'

He found a good place and plugged in the camera.

Carson Clay was ready to film *again*. But now there was a different problem. There was no explosion because the explosion machine wasn't on. And the machine wasn't on because Mr Bean plugged his video camera in!

'Stop!' Clay was very angry now. 'Where's my explosion? I want my explosion!'

Now Mr Bean's video camera was ready. He plugged the explosion machine in again.

'What's the problem?' shouted Carson Clay. 'I want my …'

BOOM!
Mr Bean wasn't there now. He was already on the road.

***

Mr Bean did not know it, but his face was now on French television.

'The police are looking for the son of a famous Russian film-maker,' said the man on television. There was a photo of Stepan on the screen. 'Someone saw the boy with this man.'

Now there was a picture of an English man on the screen. A man with a funny face.

It was Mr Bean.

CHAPTER 8
The long drive

Mr Bean was happy because a car stopped for him. He was *very* happy because it was like his little car in England!

The driver was Sabine, the actress from Carson Clay's film. She remembered Mr Bean.

'I'm going to Cannes,' she said in French with a smile.

Mr Bean didn't understand everything, but he heard the word 'Cannes'.

'Cannes! Yes, Cannes!'

They started the long drive.

'Where are you from?' asked Sabine in French. 'You're not Spanish or Italian. Are you Russian?'

Mr Bean didn't understand this, but he answered, '*Oui.*'

The woman said in French. 'I'm Sabine. And you?'

'Bean.'

Mr Bean liked the sound of the two names together. He said them a lot. 'Sabine, Bean, Sabine, Bean, Sabine …'

'I'm going to Cannes for the film festival,' said Sabine. 'I'm an actress. I'm in a film by Carson Clay. People are going to see it at the festival for the first time. After that I'm going to be a big star! It's exciting!'

Mr Bean didn't understand a word, but he smiled.

After a few minutes, Sabine stopped the car at a café. Mr Bean sat at a table and waited for her.

He looked around and suddenly he saw a big smile. It was Stepan, the Russian boy! But how did he get here?

'I didn't get on the bus,' said Stepan in Russian. 'I went with the musicians in their car!'

The musicians from that little town were here! They started to play music and Stepan started to dance. Mr Bean danced, too.

Sabine was very surprised to see them together.

✱✱✱

Now there were three people in the little green car – Sabine, Mr Bean, and Stepan. But language was a problem for them.

'Is he your son?' Sabine asked in French.

'*Oui*,' said Mr Bean.

'Is she your girlfriend?' Stepan asked in Russian.

'*Oui*,' said Mr Bean. He didn't understand any of this, but he didn't care. 'Soon I'm going to be on the beach,' he thought.

It was night now and Sabine was very tired. But they were still far from Cannes. Mr Bean started to drive. He was very tired, but he did not stop. He wanted to see that beach!

Mr Bean drove all night.

CHAPTER 9
At the cinema

A lot of people were at the Cannes Film Festival. They all wanted to see the film stars and film-makers when they arrived at the festival.

One of the films was by Carson Clay. A lot of people were in the cinema. One of the people was Stepan's father. He was there because he was a famous film-maker.

Before his film, Clay talked to the people in the cinema. 'This film is for all of us,' he said. 'It is beautiful and true.'

The film started with these words:

CARSON CLAY in A FILM BY CARSON CLAY
WRITER – CARSON CLAY

* * *

The little car was very near Cannes now and Sabine wanted to put on a new dress for the festival. Mr Bean stopped at a café.

But as they left, Sabine looked up at the television … and saw her own face. Then she saw a photo of Mr Bean. The man on the television was talking about Stepan!

She ran out to the car, angry now.

'You are not a Russian,' she said to Mr Bean in English.

'*Non*.'

'And you are not this boy's father.'

'*Non*.'

'You're English.'

Mr Bean still answered in French. '*Oui*.'

'All of France is looking for you!' shouted Sabine. 'And now they are looking for me! Who are you? Where are you going?'

This was easy. 'The beach,' said Mr Bean.

* * *

In the dark cinema, Carson Clay looked up happily
at the screen. He loved this! But the other people in the
cinema weren't so happy. Clay's black-and-white film was
long and boring. Nothing happened in it.

* * *

The police stopped Sabine's car. Sabine had a lot of
different clothes in the car. Now Mr Bean and Sabine had
some of those clothes on.
'This is my daughter,' said Sabine in French.
Stepan smiled at the policemen. He had long hair now.
'And … this is my mother,' said Sabine.
Mr Bean had on a black dress.

'Hello,' said the police.

But Mr Bean didn't understand.

'*Gracias*,' he said.

'She's Spanish,' said Sabine quickly.

She pulled out her ticket. 'I must go to the cinema,' she said. 'The film is already on. I'm not going to see my part!'

'We can help,' said the police.

And so Sabine's little car followed the police car all the way to the cinema.

Sabine ran inside with her ticket. Mr Bean and Stepan wanted to go in, too, because Stepan's father was in there! But they didn't have tickets.

CHAPTER 10
The beach!

Mr Bean and Stepan went through the back door into the cinema.

'Stop!' said a man in French. 'Where are you going?'

Mr Bean still had the dress on. He smiled at the man … and then hit him on the head with his bag!

He and Stepan ran into the cinema. Carson Clay's terrible film was still on the big screen.

'Stay here,' Mr Bean told Stepan. 'I'm going to find your father.'

He started to look around the dark cinema. He didn't find him, but he saw Sabine.

'Look,' she said. 'This is my part in the film!'

They both looked up at the screen. Carson Clay was in the film and a woman was behind him – Sabine! She walked up to him and then – nothing! Sabine had no words in the film!

'I'm not in the film!' said Sabine, angrily.

Mr Bean didn't like this. Sabine was his friend and she wanted to be a film star. Then he had an idea …

***

People in the cinema looked at their watches. 'When is this film going to end?' some thought. Some people closed their eyes and tried to sleep.

Suddenly the film on the screen changed. Now it was Sabine, in colour, with a big smile on her face. But how?

Bean! Mr Bean was in the projector room! He plugged his video camera into the projector. Now his film was on the big screen, not Carson's!

The picture on the big screen changed again. Now it

was Sabine in her little green car! Mr Bean was there, too. The people in the cinema still heard Carson Clay's words, but they watched Mr Bean's film!

In the cinema, Sabine was very surprised. Carson Clay was surprised, too … and angry. He ran to the projection room.

'Open this door!' he shouted.

On the big screen, Mr Bean did his dance for money in the little town. Then he was a German soldier … Then he was with Sabine …

Carson Clay ran into the projector room, but Mr Bean wasn't there now. He was back in the cinema. He walked across the backs of people's chairs and tried to run away.

He stopped at the front of the cinema and turned around.

'Stop!' shouted Stepan's father. 'He took my son!'

'No!' shouted Sabine. 'He didn't!'

And then Stepan walked out. The people in the cinema loved this! They were on their feet. Stepan ran into his father's arms.

Now Carson Clay was at the front of the cinema, next to Mr Bean, and he looked very angry. Then he heard the people in the cinema. They were shouting his name. They loved his film!

So he didn't hit Mr Bean. He smiled and took his hand.

***

Everyone was happy now … Everyone liked Carson Clay's new film. Sabine was a new star. Stepan was back with his father.

But what about Mr Bean? He still wanted to do one thing. He walked out of the cinema.

There was a busy street, but Mr Bean did not see the cars. He only cared about one thing – the beach!

And suddenly, it was there! He was at the beach in Cannes! Soon all his friends from the cinema were there, too.

Mr Bean smiled. What a holiday!

Meet Mr Bean

People in Britain first saw Mr Bean on TV in 1990. Mr Bean was different because the actor, Rowan Atkinson, didn't speak very often. Because of this, people enjoyed Mr Bean in other countries, too, like France, Italy, Greece and Spain. But who is Mr Bean?

* He lives alone in a small flat in London.

* He usually wears the same clothes: a jacket and a red tie.

* He drives an old Mini. Mr Bean loves his little car!

* Rowan Atkinson says Bean is a 'child in a man's body'. He isn't always nice.

* Life is never easy for Mr Bean. He finds problems everywhere.

The lives of Mr Bean

Mr Bean is a star on film and television.

Television: Fourteen different Mr Bean stories were on television between 1990 and 1995.

Cartoon: In 2002, there was also a cartoon of *Mr Bean* on television. The same actor, Rowan Atkinson, was the voice of Mr Bean.

Film: The first Mr Bean film was in 1997: *Bean – The Ultimate Disaster Movie*. In the film, Mr Bean goes to Los Angeles for a job and stays with an American family. The second film, *Mr Bean's Holiday*, was in cinemas ten years after the first film! People watched it all over the world.

> Do you like Mr Bean? Do you think he's funny? Why/why not?

Books: There are a lot of *Mr Bean* comics and books. One of them is all about France!

Mr Bean speaks!

We asked Mr Bean some questions about his holiday in France.

Why did you go on holiday to France?

All this English rain, rain, rain, rain and more rain!

Did you like French food?

Yes, but next time I'm taking a bag of sandwiches.

What are your favourite clothes?

My left shoe.

Why?

It follows my right shoe very well.

What makes you angry?

All these stupid questions!

Mr Bean has problems in the kitchen!

What do these words mean? You can use your dictionary.
sandwich   cartoon   actor

The Stars

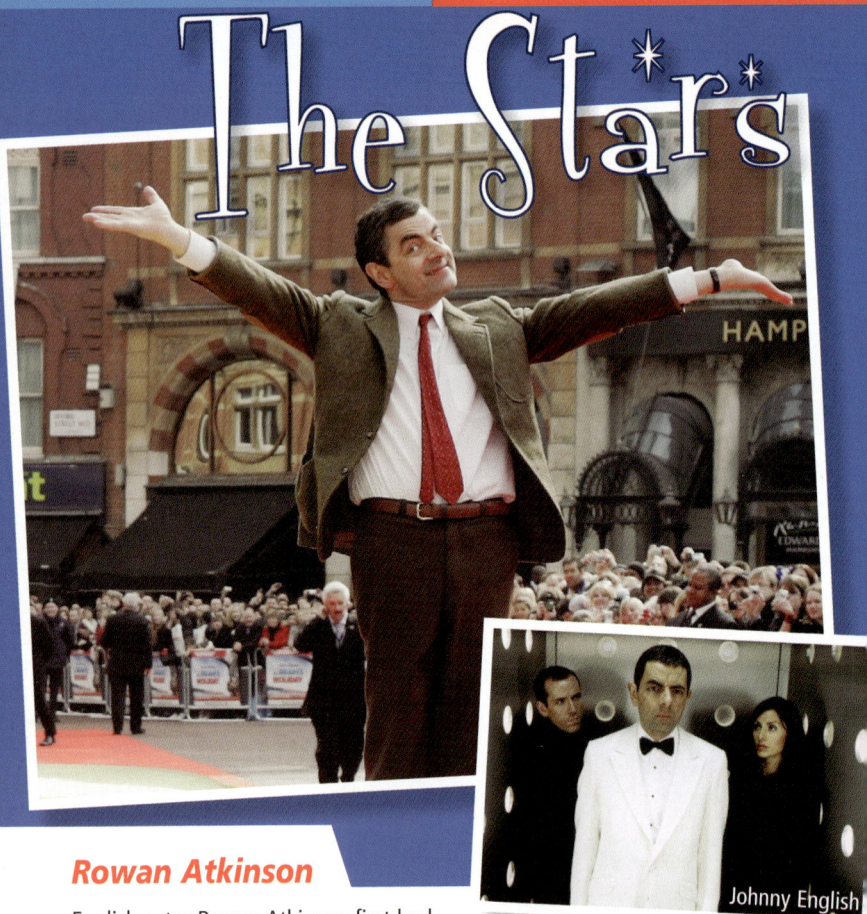

Johnny English

Rowan Atkinson

English actor Rowan Atkinson first had the idea for *Mr Bean* when he was a student in the 1970s. Then in 1990, *Mr Bean* came on TV for the first time. Before *Mr Bean*, Rowan was famous for other television programmes. One of them was *Blackadder*. Each programme was about a different time in British history. Rowan played Blackadder and helped to write the first programmes. They were very funny – British people loved them!

Film Star

✳ Rowan Atkinson acted in other films like *Four Weddings and a Funeral*.

✳ He was also the bird Zazu in the 1994 Walt Disney film, *The Lion King*.

✳ In 1983, he had a small part in a James Bond film, *Never Say Never Again*. Later, in 2003, he was *Johnny English* – a funny James Bond!

Meet Rowan Atkinson

We talked to Rowan about *Mr Bean* and *Mr Bean's Holiday*.

Do people know Mr Bean all around the world?

Yes! He's big in Japan and he's very big in Brazil. I was in a small place in Africa a few years ago. There was just one black-and-white television with a video player. And *Mr Bean* was on. Everyone watched it!

Why did you wait so long before you made a second Mr Bean film?

We made the first film in 1997. After that, I wanted to do something different. I did *Johnny English*. We had an idea for a second Mr Bean film, *Mr and Mrs Bean*. But then we had the idea of Mr Bean on holiday. We all liked that.

Why does Mr Bean go to France?

France is good because Mr Bean can't speak the language. We liked that idea. Most of the words in the film are Russian or French. Also, with a holiday, Mr Bean can be in a lot of different places and have a lot of funny problems.

Do you enjoy playing Mr Bean?

Yes, I do. And I know him very well, so it's easy. He's a child! But I don't always enjoy filming. The other actors can help, but in a film like this, Mr Bean *must* be funny. That can be very difficult sometimes.

Is it easy to play Mr Bean?

No, not always. He moves a lot so you have to be fit. When I was younger, it was easier!

Is this the end of Mr Bean?

Probably . . . but never say never!

> **Which actors and TV programmes do you find funny?**

The other actors

✱ American actor **Willem Dafoe** plays Carson Clay. Dafoe was also in the first *Spiderman* film.

✱ The film-makers spoke to lots of young actors for the part of Stepan. They wanted him to speak an East European language. Young actor **Max Baldry** is part-English and part-Russian. He now lives in Britain.

✱ **Emma de Caunes** plays Sabine. Like Sabine, Emma is French, and she can speak English.

> **Look up these words in your dictionary.**
> act / actor   fit   history   programme

Mr Bean's France

Mr Bean makes careful plans for his holiday. First, he takes the train – the Eurostar – from London to Paris. It takes about 2.5 hours. It goes under the sea between England and France. It arrives at one of Paris's six train stations. The train to Cannes goes from one of the other stations.

Mr Bean in Paris

In his taxi (to the wrong part of Paris) Mr Bean sees these famous places.

The Louvre is one of the most famous art galleries in the world. You can see the Mona Lisa here.

The Eiffel Tower is the most famous building in Paris. Six million people go up the tower every year.

The beautiful church **Notre Dame** is over 650 years old.

The Eiffel Tower *The Louvre*

PARIS

Notre Dame

Paris to Cannes

The train from Paris to Cannes is a TGV, one of the fastest trains in the world. Its name means 'fast train' in French. It can go over 300 kilometres an hour. The train from Paris to Cannes takes under six hours to go 891 kilometres. Mr Bean takes a lot longer than this!

Mr Bean is not the only British person on holiday in France. Every year, 12 million British people go to France on holiday. British children learn French at school, so they know more than Mr Bean's two words! But, like Mr Bean, many British people cannot speak French very well.

Cannes

Cannes is a lovely town on the Mediterranean sea. It has got beautiful beaches, but the town is most famous for its film festival.

For 12 days every May, Cannes is the centre of the film world. There is a competition and judges choose the year's best film. In *Mr Bean's Holiday*, Stepan's father is one of these judges.

Most of the films at the festival are not in the competition. Film-makers and film stars from all over the world come to Cannes because they want to sell their new films.

You are going to France for a short holiday. Do you want to go to Paris or Cannes?

What do these words mean? You can use your dictionary.
art gallery   church   judge   sea   tower

CHAPTERS 1–3

Before you read

1 Look at these words. You can use a dictionary.

actor   church   map   tie   vending machine

Which one . . .

a) is a building?

b) can people wear?

c) is in films?

d) has got food or drink in it?

e) is usually paper?

2 Complete the sentences with these words. You can use a dictionary.

compass   competition   prize

a) There is an exciting … in today's newspaper.

b) I want to win the first … – it's a new car!

c) A … is useful when you are walking in the country.

3 What do you think?

a) Mr Bean's "dream holiday" is in France / America / Britain.

b) Mr Bean goes to France by car / train / boat.

c) He goes with a friend / with his family / alone.

4 What is your "dream holiday"?

After you read

5 Are these sentences true or false? Correct the false sentences.

a) Mr Bean has got ticket number 616 in the competition.

b) The first prize is a holiday in Paris.

c) Mr Bean goes to Paris by train.

d) He can speak French very well.

e) A taxi takes him to the second station in Paris.

6 Answer the questions.

a) How does Mr Bean arrive at the second station?

b) Who is Carson Clay?

c) What takes Mr Bean's tie?

d) What country is Stepan from?

e) Why is Stepan unhappy on the train?

CHAPTERS 4–6

Before you read

7 Circle the right answer.
   a) Where does a ticket inspector work?
   i) in a bank   **ii)** on a train   **iii)** in a restaurant
   b) What do people usually keep in a wallet?
   i) money   **ii)** food   **iii)** pens
   c) What do musicians do?
   i) play music   **ii)** listen to music   **iii)** sell music

8 Look at the words and answer the questions.
   chicken   moped   tank
   Which one . . .
   a) can you eat?
   b) is very dangerous?
   c) can you ride?

9 What do you think?
   Mr Bean and Stepan are at a station in France. What are they going to do now?

After you read

10 Correct these sentences.
   a) Stepan can't read the telephone number because Mr Bean's hand is over the last two numbers.
   b) Mr Bean leaves his bag at the station.
   c) When Mr Bean and Stepan act the story of the music, people give them food.
   d) They buy train tickets with the money.
   e) Mr Bean takes a moped and follows the chickens.
   f) A big bus drover on top of his bicycle.

11 Answer these questions.
   a) Why does Mr Bean follow the chicken?
   b) Why doesn't he ride the bicycle back to the town?
   c) Why can't Mr Bean take the big man's moped?
   d) Why does he start to walk to Cannes?

CHAPTERS 7–10

Before you read

12 Match the words with the sentences.

explosion festival plug it in projector screen soldier

a) A TV has got one of these.
b) You can find this machine in a cinema.
c) This is very loud.
d) This person fights for his or her country.
e) You can see a lot of films, plays or music at this.
f) You have to do this to a TV before you can watch it.

13 What do you think?
Look at the pictures in chapters 7–10.
a) Why are there soldiers (p21)?
b) Who is Mr Bean in a car with (p24)?
c) Why are Mr Bean and Stepan wearing different clothes (p27)?

Now read and find the answers.

After you read

14 Answer the questions. Who . . .
a) wakes up and sees German soldiers?
b) is making a film in France?
c) wants to be a big star?
d) was with some musicians in their car?
e) goes to the projector room and changes the film?

15 Put these sentences in order.
a) Mr Bean meets Stepan again.
b) Stepan sees his father again.
c) Mr Bean is on the beach.
d) Sabine goes into the cinema.
e) Carson Clay sends Mr Bean away.
f) Mr Bean drives all night.
g) Mr Bean changes the film.
h) Sabine stops her car for Mr Bean.

16 What do you think?
a) Is everyone happy at the end?
b) Do you like the end? Why/Why not?